AFTER THE SONGS WERE SUNG

John J. Marnien

AFTER THE SONGS WERE SUNG

Text by John J. Marnien. Jr.

Poems by Peter John Ebbecke

Jemsco Publishing, LLC

Copyright ©2021 by John J. Marnien, Jr.

All rights reserved. No part of this book shall be reproduced or transmitted in any form or by any means, electronic, mechanical, magnetic, photographic including photocopying, recording or by any information and retrieval system, without prior written permission of the publisher. No patent liability is assumed with respect to the use of the information contained herein. Although every precaution has been taken in the preparation of this book, the publisher and author assume no responsibility for errors or omissions. Neither is any liability assumed for damages resulting from the use of the information contained therein.

ISBN 978-1-7377701-2-1

Cover design and Art ©2021 by John J. Marnien, Jr.

All photographs are from the Marnien Family Collection

Published by:
    Jemsco Publishing, LLC
    P. O. Box 443
    Fairless Hills, Pa 19030

Printed in the United States of America,. Published September 2022

This book is dedicated to Harry Himes, Rosesylvia McDonald and Cynara Himes who encouraged the development of this book.

It is also dedicated to the many family members whose lives share in the legacy of Peter John Ebbecke.

In particular, it is dedicated to my mother, Bernice Marnien, nee Ebbecke who preserved and handed down to me the copies of Uncle Pete's poetry and so many of the family stories.

Particular appreciation is due to my wife, MaryEllen who assisted and encouraged me throughout the development of

    AFTER THE SONGS WERE SUNG

AFTER THE SONGS WERE SUNG

Before the Songs Began

No individual is born into a vacuum. Most of us are born and grow up within a defined family. All of us are products of a particular time and situation in history that influences who and what we are.

It is difficult to look back on the life of Peter John Ebbecke from our current circumstances. We are left to our own memories which have grown somewhat vague and otherwise uncertain. It can also be a difficult challenge to separate the memories and stories of our family from those which are peculiarly our own. It is hard to separate recollections of our own experiences from the tales that our parents related to us as we grew.

Added to that is the realization that our other relatives have their own perspective. Sometimes they enforce our observations and sometimes their view is different from our own.

AFTER THE SONGS WERE SUNG

My principal objective is to preserve and share what can be recaptured of the life of a particular uncle who had a significant influence on myself and on many of my cousins.

Peter's mother, Agnes Walsh, was born in Waterford, Ireland to Peter Joseph Walsh and Margaret Cummins Walsh. This has been verified by accessing her birth record in Ireland. In 1888, as a young woman, Agnes was sent by her parents to resettle in the United States. She sailed on the immigrant ship, the Pennland. The manifest notes that Agnes' fare was paid by her aunt Mary. She came to live with these relatives, Joseph P. Liston, his wife Mary Ellen Walsh and their daughter Georgina. The Liston family had moved to the United States in 1886. The plan was that once Agnes was established in the United States, the other family members could also relocate. They are all listed in the 1900 Census which also notes that Agnes was employed as a "spooler". Joseph Liston is listed as a laborer.

AFTER THE SONGS WERE SUNG

Georgina and Agnes

Immigrants arriving in Philadelphia were frequently disembarked in Tacony. That town at the time was economically divided by the railroad tracks. Typically, new residents settled on the river side of the tracks. As they acquired sufficient wealth, they relocated to the better side – the area surrounding St. Leo's parish church and school.

The primary work site for men was on the north end of the town where the principal company was Disston Saw. Women were frequently employed on the southern side where there were a few garment companies. One such company was the Fine Art Lace Company owned by the Mehler family, cousins of Harry Adam Ebbecke.

Agnes settled on the New Jersey side of the river and went to work in a garment factory. A family tradition was that she was so small that she had to stand upon a box to reach the clothes that she was sorting. That story was proven in error by the referenced census. Over the years Agnes continued to deduct years from her age making necessary the tale that she began working in the garment factory at the age of 4.

Harry Adam Ebbecke and his family had migrated at an earlier date. Harry's father is identified on some documents as Henry Adam Ebbecke and elsewhere as Harry. Oral tradition insists that his first name was Adam. More certain is that he was a shoemaker specializing in making women's shoes. (The problem over the correct first name for males in the family is further demonstrated by the fact that Harry Adam Ebbecke appears on his marriage certificate as simply "Henry Ebbecke").

AFTER THE SONGS WERE SUNG

The Ebbecke family was strongly linked to the nearby Children's Home, Saint Vincent's. Behind the main building there is a small cemetery where many Ebbeckes were buried.

Harry Adam Ebbecke had been an insurance salesman. He first became acquainted with Agnes Walsh when he called at the family home to try to sell an insurance policy. Attracted to Agnes, Harry returned again and again to the home on the same pretext. Eventually, Harry and Agnes courted and were married.

Harry and Agnes were dedicated to having a son named Harry. Of their first five children, three were named Harry. Two of the Harrys died in their infancy. Another child, Benjamin Franklin Ebbecke, also died as an infant.

Harry and Agnes retold the story that they happened to be in the room with one infant at the moment of his death. They observed something that looked to them like a white handkerchief rise from the crib and ascend until it disappeared through the ceiling.

Far down the line of children, twin boys were born on November 20, 1919. These were fraternal twins, Paul George and Peter John. It is Peter John whose life and poetry are the prime subjects of this book.

The children were born into a harsh era of our history. The United States had struggled through World War I. The roaring twenties then led the society quickly into the Great Depression.

At one point, Harry and Agnes decided that things might go better for them if they moved the family to Florida.

One day, the children came home from school and were told to leave their books by the door and get into the car. While this scene was playing out, one of the older daughters arrived at the house. She and her husband had an argument, and she was coming over with her child to see her parents. Her father, Harry, told her that it was all right if she wanted to talk, but that she should get into the car. The rest of the family got into the vehicle and they drove away with the daughter and child in tow. According to the story as it came down to me, the next thing that her husband heard, his wife and child had been relocated to Florida.

On the way south, an older brother shared the responsibility of driving the car. One day, he fell asleep at the wheel. The car left the road, passed through a farmer's property, and fortunately came to a stop in a haystack. Quicky freeing the vehicle, the family got back on the road and proceeded on their journey.

As it turned out, life in Florida was not an improvement over their home in Philadelphia. I was frequently told how the children would come home from school by walking along the railroad tracks. Often, potatoes that had fallen from the railroad cars could be found on the tracks. That evening they would have the potatoes for dinner. The following morning, they would have the peels of the potatoes fried for their breakfast. In retelling the story, it was never clear to me exactly how long the family remained down south.

AFTER THE SONGS WERE SUNG

Peter by the steering wheel with Bernice in the center of the family car. Paul appears to be about to bail out. Behind him are Vincent and Peggy.

It would have been tough going to Florida with them and the rest of the family.

AFTER THE SONGS WERE SUNG

The Beginning of the Songs

Just as there is uncertainty about when the family moved to Florida, there is no clear information about when they returned to the Philadelphia area.

Another item that is not certain is exactly when music became an important part of the everyday life of the Ebbeckes.

At some time, Bernice and Peter became well acquainted with the songs from the earlier century as well as the music of the 1900s through the 1920s.

As evidenced by the advertisement and my mother's notation on page 14, Bernice and Peter had learned to dance together well enough that they frequently won neighborhood dance contests.

They were appearing as "child singers" at the Green Lantern Grill in north Philadelphia. Additionally, they were regular singers on radio station WTEL. On Sundays they were normally heard on the radio on the Horn and Hardart's

AFTER THE SONGS WERE SUNG

Children's Hour. Every Saturday they appeared at the Northeastern Theater in Wissinoming.

Somehow, Agnes Ebbecke was getting them seen and heard at these venues. To be appearing there with the apparent regularity indicated, they had to be somehow transported to these establishments. Considering that Agnes never learned to drive, that would have been quite an accomplishment.

There was never any indication that either Bernice or Peter ever had any dance and/or singing lessons. Added to the mysteries is that at some point Pete learned to play the piano.

It would be too easy to simply say that they were somehow "naturals" when it came to entertainment. However, there were a number of other members of the family that had definite associations with the arts and entertainment industry. How or when the associations were made, or how so many were adept at so much remains a mystery to others while it was just accepted as normalcy within the family.

AFTER THE SONGS WERE SUNG

For instance, there was an uncle in the family who owned a music store. That operation was a sideline; his main occupation was being a musician and song writer. He wrote the words and the music to many songs. There are songs that are known to family members to this day that seem to have originated with that uncle.

The circumstance was repeated in our own lives when our children became confused about some of the songs that they and all of their friends were familiar with but that others did not know. It was resolved when my wife and I explained the situation to them. The songs in question were songs that my wife and I had written and taught to our children. They in turn had taught them to their neighborhood friends. The songs are now being sung to our great grandson.

Another example is that my Aunt Agnes introduced me to the harmonica and later to the guitar. I never have had any idea why she possessed these instruments or how she had learned to play them.

AFTER THE SONGS WERE SUNG

In turn, I learned to play them. I performed with the guitar for many years and taught literally hundreds of students. I have dozens of copyrighted songs but still have had little formal music instruction myself.

As the radio industry changed over the years, Peter Ebbecke was involved and associated with many of the developments. He performed on the radio and in person as Peter Fredericks. He had several friends who were involved with radio station WJMJ in Philadelphia.

Later, Pete was the Record Librarian for WDAS. While there, Pete worked with a performer, Joseph Niagra. Eventually, Peter introduced his sister Margaret "Peggy" to Niagra. Later, Joe and Peggy were married. Joe's show always opened with an old song, "Peg of My Heart" for his wife Peggy. My Uncle Joe and Aunt Peggy lived at 758 Carver Street and we lived a few doors away at 766.

Incidentally, my Uncle Joe's car was the first privately owned vehicle that I ever rode in.

AFTER THE SONGS WERE SUNG

Peggy Ebbecke and Joseph Niagra
Wedding picture
(One of the few left to me by my
Mother, Bernice.)

AFTER THE SONGS WERE SUNG

A newspaper ad concerning an appearance of Peter and Bernice (Ebbecke) – WTEL Child singers.
On the side of the ad are handwritten notes from
Bernice Ebbecke about their performance schedule.

AFTER THE SONGS WERE SUNG

The Songs Go to War

At one point, the family rented a mansion on Route 13 just north of Philadelphia. Harry Ebbecke's ventures must have been doing very well about that time. The mansion was a beautiful home on a large piece of property near St. Dominic's Cemetery. On the grounds were many apple trees. This fact motivated some of the boys in the family with a unique business opportunity. With the apples being free, they determined that they would go into business making and selling apple cider. They were ambitious and completely undeterred by the fact that none of them had any idea how to make apple cider.

Nevertheless, they proceeded with their new venture. Soon the apples were beginning to ripen. Clearly, the first step was to gather in the fresh fruit. For some reason that remains obscure, they believed that the ideal storage area for the fruit would be in an available second floor bedroom. With the fervency of new business owners, the boys began collecting the apples and transporting them to the bedroom.

Over a few days the apple pile deepened. With the weather still being warm, the apples began to further ripen, and the air quality began to deteriorate. Gradually, the realization settled in that the planning may not have been sufficient.

It must have been a sight that was talked about by the neighbors for years. Without any more viable solution, the boys began to shovel the now-reeking apple mush out of the second story window. It has not come down to us who the primary mover of the apple plot was, but thankfully the removal of the apples was successful.

It is not known how close to the moving of the apples was the subsequent moving of the Ebbeckes.

Ironically, the location near the cemetery was not far from the place where some years before the body was found.

AFTER THE SONGS WERE SUNG

The body in that case belonged to a young girl who had been kidnapped and killed. Her remains had been found along Neshaminy Creek.

At the time of the crime, the Ebbecke family lived near the Bridge Street terminal in Frankford. Two young sisters were kidnapped, and Agnes Ebbecke and her children, Rosesylvia, Edwin, and little Agnes were witnesses to the abduction. Edwin had even approached the criminal who had the girls in his car. Edwin had been cursed at and told to go away.

Largely due their testimony, the criminal was captured and successfully prosecuted. The Ebbecke family was vital to the process.

The criminal was executed about 18 months after his conviction.

Years later, the family was again living in the Frankford section of Philadelphia and World War II had begun without them. The United States might have missed the beginning of the conflict but was going to swiftly be brought into the hostilities.

AFTER THE SONGS WERE SUNG

The ancestry of the Ebbecke family serving their country extended from the early days of the Revolutionary War when at least one of its ancestors had taken part in the invasion of Canada. (An ancestry chart appears following this page). During the main part of the war there were three generations of the family serving in the conflict at the same time.

Harry Adam Ebbecke was a veteran of the Spanish American War.

Along with many of the other members of the family, Peter John Ebbecke became a veteran of World War II.

Fortunately, all the members of the Ebbecke family returned from serving the country without any serious injury.

Somehow during those years, a great body of memorable music was produced that included many of our classic love ballads.

AFTER THE SONGS WERE SUNG

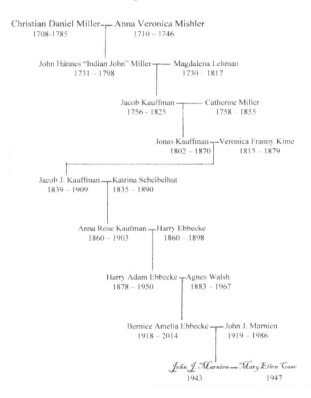

Family Ancestry Chart beginning with 3 ancestors from the American Revolution. The author is the bottom entry on the chart. Peter John Ebbecke was the brother of Bernice Ebbecke.

AFTER THE SONGS WERE SUNG

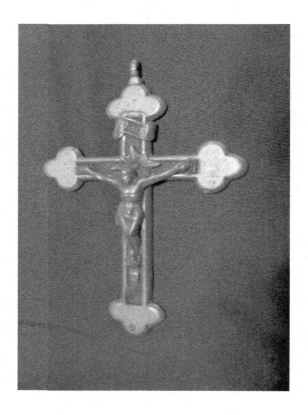

This is the Crucifix that Uncle Pete gave to me. I believe that it was from his days in the seminary. Pete insisted that there were so many blessings placed on it that if one died with it in their hand, they would go straight to heaven.

AFTER THE SONGS WERE SUNG

The Songs Mature

In the years after World War II, Pete's life gradually changed, taking on new dimensions.

Always rather serious and with a strong religious background, Pete was drawn to consider whether he had a vocation to the priesthood. I do not know how long Pete was involved with the seminary except that there was a connection and for some time he investigated whether he was called. During that time, he apparently wore a crucifix as part of his attire. He kept that cross for many years until one day he gave it to me. A picture of that cross is on the previous page. During his years in the seminary Peter became proficient in both Latin and Greek.

Around the same time, his twin brother Paul was drawn to become a brother in an order of the Church.

Both twins eventually left the seminary and returned to the secular life.

AFTER THE SONGS WERE SUNG

For Pete, that involved working daytime to support himself and his mother. For many years he worked for Social Security. Later he went to work for a Philadelphia radio station WDAS. He continued to play the piano and pursue his love of performing on radio, in local clubs – wherever he could entertain others with the music he loved.

Peter also shared with his numerous nephews and nieces his many other interests. With some of us, he shared his love of and knowledge about the use of Latin. Others would be amazed with his abilities in the use of mathematics. I watched him on numerous occasions buy many items at a store and calculate the total amount due faster than the clerk using the calculator.

With many others he shared his love of reading, in particular the reading of the classic novels.

At family gatherings and celebrations, Pete could be counted upon to control the music playing at the party or affair.

AFTER THE SONGS WERE SUNG

Invariably, there would come a time for live presentations by various individuals, spontaneous duets, or assorted entertainment by those present.

Christmas was always a special occasion with Peter. At some point he would get everyone's attention and explain that it was not truly Christmas to him until he heard "Silent Night". Pete would then put on a recording and begin playing it. Within a few seconds the song would be interrupted by someone who just could not resist talking above the music. Ironically, that person was always Pete himself. I watched many a Christmas party come to an end without Pete ever hearing "Silent Night".

I made several recordings from the various parties. It is a joy listening once again to my aunts and uncles, father and mother singing along or in duets or other spontaneous groups.

AFTER THE SONGS WERE SUNG

Pete performing at a party.

AFTER THE SONGS WERE SUNG

Songs Without Music

It is not clear when Pete became interested in writing poetry. Neither is it clear how many poems he may have written. The following is the statement that my mother, Bernice, gave me with the copies of the poems that were in her possession.

"All the following poems were written by my brother, Pete. He suffered from throat cancer and spent many months is an army Rehabilitation Center in Virginia.

Some of his poems reflect his thoughts while knowing he was dying.

He had an extremely high I.Q. You will notice this by some of the words he uses, words that most people never heard of. He had a beautiful singing voice and was a great piano player. He and I won many prizes dancing together at block parties.

AFTER THE SONGS WERE SUNG

I was closer to Pete than I was to any of my other brothers and sisters.

He passed away on June 21, 1970.

Bernice Marnien"

There is no indication that I could find indicating whether any of his poems were published anywhere. He seems to have reserved them to send to certain family members.

From what I have been able to determine, the following are the only works that have survived. If other family members discover more in their possession, and if they give me copies, those works may be added to a future edition of this book.

Until then, enjoy the poems of Peter John Ebbecke.

AFTER THE SONGS WERE SUNG

A PRAYER

God grant me the strength to accept each day

And what may fall therein

To be humble and pure and with your grace

Resist all temptation and sin.

Pilot me, god on this road of life

Which at times can be weary and steep.

Let my faith in Your Love and Hope in Your Light

Peace and harmony verily reap.

Help me dear Lord, in all future trials

To be tolerant, patient, and wise.

Let me rest secure in Your Omnipotent love

Where only true happiness lies.

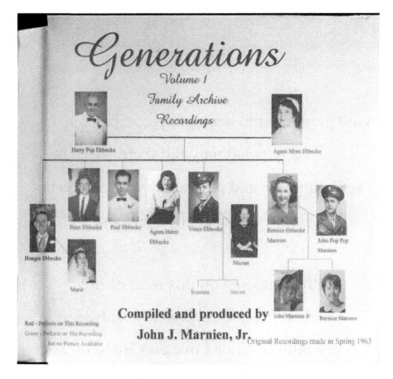

Some of the holiday parties that were hosted by Pete were taped. Those recordings were later converted into CD discs. Their future is now better assured through the auspices of the Jemsco Publishing, LLC and the Family Archive Recording Series.

AFTER THE SONGS WERE SUNG

AGENDA

From the bright rim of the propitious morning
To the blunt edge of the tenebrous night,
I gather all thoughts for the pleasure of taking
Put all that is negative out into flight.

In the interim I'll dispel all that is dismal.
Tread the bright line that leads me to right.
Foster kind deeds of a wonderful making
Put all that is vacuous out of my sight.

With the coming of night and its dark shades calling
I'll renew all the hopes that I had from the start –
Repose in a most agreeable fashion
Happy in spirit – contented at heart.

Peter's sister Agnes who introduced the author to music by giving John his first musical instruments.

AFTER THE SONGS WERE SUNG

BATTLE

How many times have you made a promise
And vowed to keep it with honest intent,
When faced with the force of an old-age passion
From which you have prayed for a fast relent?

How often with all the might that was in you,
You fought to defeat it at any cost,
When the very nature you relied on would weaken
And you thought that the cause was undoubtedly lost?

How lucky you were to have such a challenge!
Temptation is sly – a formidable foe.
But the more you meet it in daily battle,
The chance for your victory increases, you know.

AFTER THE SONGS WERE SUNG

Above is Pete's sister Rosesylvia. She was also the godmother of the author. She married Francis Himes who was the first cousin of her sister Mercedes' husband Francis Walton.

AFTER THE SONGS WERE SUNG

CONFESSION

Digging down deep in the cave of memory
This is what I find
I mingled too long in the joys of fancy –
Overlooked the sublime.

Probing too far in the halls of mystery
Not being satisfied –
I surpassed myself in a futile fashion
Leaving the best aside.

Searching the core of my spirit's dwelling
Longing for peace
O God, from the chains of my relentless desires
Grant me release!

AFTER THE SONGS WERE SUNG

Marie and Edwin Ebbecke's Wedding

Peter is the third person from the left in the back row. Uncle Steven Walsh, Mom Ebbecke's brother, is the third person from the right in the back row. Uncle Steve also came to the United States from Ireland.

AFTER THE SONGS WERE SUNG

DECLARATION

No pessimist – I
With hope as sure as eagle wings
I choose my flight
Then fly.

My sinecure – for me
I prefer to perform my diurnal work
Sedulously
As a bee.
No leader, pray indeed
I battle too much opposition
To beat –
The day's speed.

No encomium – please
I'll merit only what is due me
Then happily rest –
At ease.

No epitaph – at last
Words carved from silent stone
For future eyes
Can never tell my past.

AFTER THE SONGS WERE SUNG

Above is the immigrant ship the Pennland on which Agnes Walsh came to the United States age 16.

AFTER THE SONGS WERE SUNG

THOUGHTS

Out of pain
Happiness grows.
There is endless beauty
In heavy snows.

Out of defeat
Hope is the way.
Doesn't the dawn
Announce a new day?

Out of dying
Comes a new life
After death
The soul takes its flight.

AFTER THE SONGS WERE SUNG

Pete in all his glory at the piano.

AFTER THE SONGS WERE SUNG

FRIENDSHIP

If you admire your friend – let him know it.
Delight in telling him so.
Place all his attributes out in the front
And all of his faults forgo.

Rejoice in his every victory –
Stand by if troubles ensue.
When onerous cares seem to darken his day
Give him courage to see it through.

Exemplify all that means fairness –
Set his heart's spirit aglow
Be a paragon of all that friendship implies,
And watch how the amity grows.

Thank God that you really found someone
On whom you can really depend.
For of all the wonderful joys in life –
What's comparable to having a friend?

AFTER THE SONGS WERE SUNG

Children of Harry Adam Ebbecke and Agnes May Jay Virginia Walsh

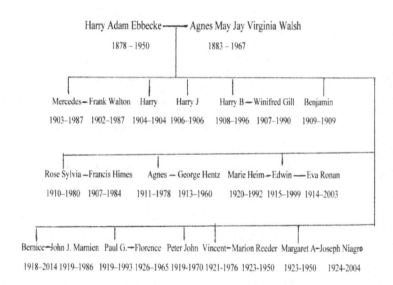

AFTER THE SONGS WERE SUNG

GARDEN OF LIFE

On my vatic tour through the garden of life,

I have such a wonderful time.

As the florescent picture presents itself,

I rejoice in the lovely design.

Culling the gems which I think are the best.

Leaving the rest to themselves.

I garner the ones that I elect to be mine,

Vase them on decorous shelves.

I ask my friends to come to my house.

The ones to whom life is not fair.

Suggest that they linger around for a chat,

Share in the fragrance there.

I smile as they gaze at the beautiful view,

Forget all their cares and strife.

I then take them down through the wonderful path

Of my wonderful garden of life.

AFTER THE SONGS WERE SUNG

Bernice Marnien (nee Ebbecke)

Bernice was Peter Ebbecke's dance partner. The two danced together and frequently won dance contests, From when they were children they regularly sang in the same venues.

She preserved the copies of Peter's poems making this document possible.

She is also the mother of the author of this book.

AFTER THE SONGS WERE SUNG

THERAPY

As I emerge from the brunt of my recent trauma
I obviate all that engenders duress.
Amenable to all that is therapeutic
I follow the regimen deemed to be best.

In my tenure carved out of daedal personae
Replete with samples of various cures.
I traipse the path of my firm endeavor,
And pray that my new-found courage endures.

Spurred by the impetus proffered by many
That I place in my book of "forget me not";
I'll merit the victory the future holds for me,
And grasp with joy the inevitable lot.

AFTER THE SONGS WERE SUNG

Paul Ebbecke was the twin brother of Peter.
They did not look alike at all.

It is interesting that when it came to singing their voices sounded very much the same.

AFTER THE SONGS WERE SUNG

YOUR GOAL

What if your dreams of yesterday
Have not been realized.
What if each plan you strove for
Never materialized.
There's always a new tomorrow,
New courage – new venture ahead;
Intrepid, dauntless, courageous
Oppose all the odds instead.
Never lose faith in the struggle,
No matter how dim the light.
The cares and worries of every day
Soon banish before the night.
Be honest, true and steadfast,
Tenacious, persistent and stout.
With hope in your heart for the future
The goal that you seek will win out.

AFTER THE SONGS WERE SUNG

Edwin Hogan Ebbecke was another brother of Peter.

Edwin was named for a wealthy relative who had no children. There was conjecture that naming Edwin after the cousin would secure some of the relative's riches.

If that was the plan it did not work.

AFTER THE SONGS WERE SUNG

A WASTED DAY

Here in the night quiescent
My thoughts seem to have full sway
I think of the day inspired.
Of deeds I let go astray.

The passing smile I'd forgotten –
A service I left undone;
An unselfish deed I might have performed,
The gain that I could have won.

The downcast look make uplifted –
Some humbled one offered some praise.
The myriad tasks of noblest kind,
Placed out in splendid arrays.

Here in the night quiescent
With my better half out in display.
I promise if I live 'til tomorrow,
I'll not waste the golden day.

AFTER THE SONGS WERE SUNG

Vincent Ebbecke as he served in WWII.

The name Vincent probably was the result of the family's long association with Sr. Vincent's Home in north Philadelphia.

AFTER THE SONGS WERE SUNG

SORROW

How to describe the weight of sorrow

How to assure the intolerable pain?

There is only the hope of a safe recovery

Out of it finding new strength again.

Who can console the one who is under

The weight of this regular pattern of life?

Be it a parent – be it a friend

Be it a brother, husband or wife.

How to explain that it's only acceptance

Can help to defeat this unfortunate blow –

To realize it's all part of God's plan

Is all that we need to know.

EASTER

Resurrexit sicut dixit

"He has risen as He said"

The bells ring out most clearly

On this bright and joyful day.

The more we read the sacred words

More blessed they become.

They signify Eternal Life

For each and everyone.

The scriptures tell the story –

The meaning they proclaim;

We will all arise miraculously

To glory in His Name.

AFTER THE SONGS WERE SUNG

REHABILITATION

Thanks to the friends who found me to be
A hopeless, disconsolate recluse.
Who discovered my dormant talent
And put it to veritable use.
Who helped me throw off the reinvents-
Self-pity, depression, and pain,
Set me to positive thinking
Helped me find hope once again.
Their efforts, counsel, and interest
Were a balm to obdurate me.
They little knew of the lethal gyves
That were slowly destroying me.
I know now that life is worth living,
They've proved it beyond any doubt
Intact, enthused, and elated
I've put all my worries to rout.

AFTER THE SONGS WERE SUNG

IF THERE WAS A WAY

If there was a way to blot out all dissension
That precipitates sorry and endless strife,
I'd give all of my efforts in infinite measure,
To devote all the rest of my natural life-
In seeing that each individual was given
That portion of life, which is really the best,
By giving a good deal of courage and wisdom
With which to be valiant and survive any test.

If there was a way to relieve the misfortune
That falls upon those who seek to do right

I'd light lanterns of faith for the hopeless millions
With fervent hope of incessant delight.
They'd live in a world of their own desire.

AFTER THE SONGS WERE SUNG

I'd exclude from them every worry and pain.
And when they grew old and felt they were wanting.
I'd augment the blessings all over again.

AFTER THE SONGS WERE SUNG

GLAMOROUS-PLUS

(to Mercedes)
Sometimes it's in the person
Sometimes it's in the name
It really makes no difference
It adds up to the same:

She would have you remember
And remember you must:
She longed to be glamorous
Glamorous-plus.

Fancy and bright her dresses should be
Add a few sequins? Yes, she'd agree.
Earrings that sparkle – accent the eyes.
Just enough make-up to prove she was wise.

All the accessories, her hats and shoes
Were always the latest, the best she could choose.
If on an occasion you asked why the fuss?
She'd say, "I want to be glamorous, glamorous-plus."

AFTER THE SONGS WERE SUNG

Fate, the old weaver, spinning the plot,
Put a crimp in her glamour in choosing her lot.
Marriage and children, year after year,
Had somewhat to do with the wear and the tear.

But now that she's older and easy on age –
You have to admit she was meant for the stage,
Sometimes she gets restless – she might even cuss.
"I was meant to glamorous, glamorous-plus."

AFTER THE SONGS WERE SUNG

Pete with two of his sisters, Mercedes on the left and Margaret on the right. Mercedes is the subject of the poem "Glamorous-Plus".

AFTER THE SONGS WERE SUNG

AFTER THE SONGS WERE SUNG

The Last Dance

Eventually, the years began to catch up with Uncle Pete. His mother Agnes had passed away. His health began to work against him as well and a long-time family malady became apparent.

Pete's grandfather had died at twenty-nine from cancer of the esophagus. His father, Harry Adam Ebbecke, died in 1950 from the same problem.

With Peter, the esophagus was still involved although in his instance the problem was his throat. His symptoms began quietly enough, but he was eventually diagnosed as having cancer of the throat. He went into a veteran's hospital for treatment and spent a long time away from Philadelphia. Eventually it appeared that Pete had successfully escaped with much of his health. Unfortunately, his cure was more apparent than it was real.

AFTER THE SONGS WERE SUNG

After a few years he was again in a hospital with a recurrence of the same illness. This time the situation was more difficult for Pete. The treatment affected his throat until he was finally no longer able to sing.

He suffered for a while with an unwelcome hoarseness.

Finally, on June 21, 1970 Uncle Peter John Ebbecke lost his final battle and returned to his Lord and his Maker.

AFTER THE SONGS WERE SUNG

AFTER THE SONGS WERE SUNG

Love,
Uncle Pete

AFTER THE SONGS WERE SUNG

AFTER THE SONGS WERE SUNG

AFTER THE SONGS WERE SUNG

Made in the USA
Middletown, DE
21 September 2022

10569604R00046